I0421639

Why Are They Like That?
Asians

*Questions you've dared to ask, answered
by real people, celebrities and experts*

A book series based on the award-winning
sharing project that's captured worldwide
attention helping people in their personal,
social and business relationships

Phillip J. Milano

For Robin, Jacob, Lucas and Ben

Publisher:
Y Forum
yforum@yforum.com

ISBN: 978-1-07-793828-1

Cover and interior layout by Sandy Weber,
Key 3 Creative, Jacksonville, Florida
Cover photo credit: Rawpixel. Stock photo for illustrative purposes
only; any person depicted is a posed model.

Content based in part on the popular Y? sharing project and Dare
to Ask column

Find out more about the author, upcoming books and speeches at
www.phillipmilano.com, facebook.com/PhillipJMilano or
@PhillipMilano.

Books In This Series

Why Are They Like That? Blacks

Why Are They Like That? Whites

Why Are They Like That? Hispanics

Why Are They Like That? Asians

Why Are They Like That? Gay Men

Why Are They Like That? Lesbians

Why Are They Like That? Women

Why Are They Like That? Men

Why Are They Like That? Rich and Poor

Why Are They Like That? Religious (or not)

Why Are They Like That? Disabled People

Why Are They Like That? Young and Old

Praise for the Y? sharing project and the book "I Can't Believe You Asked That!" (Perigee)

"Milano is quietly revolutionizing cross-cultural communication..."
- Pulitzer Prize-winning columnist Leonard Pitts

"If you've ever hesitated to ask a question because you think it might be considered insensitive or impolitic, now is your chance ... Nothing is considered out of bounds..."
- CNN Headline News

"(It) tells more about who we are and how we feel about each other than you're likely to learn from a dozen sociology texts…"
- Washington Post News Service

"Mr. Milano has dared to open the field of debate to the maximum…"
- Le Monde, Paris

"(A) remarkable contribution to cross-cultural understanding…"
- The (London) Guardian

"A truly rare achievement … has the potential to have a profound impact on the way we all see and understand each other..."
- Playboy magazine

"It's an incredible book. It diffuses everything ... Nothing is off limits, and the questions have that childlike honesty to them..."
- Dee Snider, Twisted Sister; host, "Dee Snider Radio"

"A take-no-prisoners attitude prevails between the volume's covers . . . This book is hard to put down..."
- Midwest Book Review

"A+ (highest rating)… Everything you wanted to know but were afraid to ask gets tackled here ..."
- Entertainment Weekly

CONTENTS

Introduction

Why Are They Like That? is a series of books based on an award-winning worldwide sharing project in which real people, experts and celebrities talk about things that make us different from each other. Silly things. Sad things. Funny things. Profound things.

Read with an open mind and we believe that by the time you're finished you'll have a much better understanding of how to make more and real friends, money and love. It's that simple.

Why? Because this isn't about trying to get ahead with diversity training. We are well beyond that. According to the Census Bureau, by 2050 the United States will have no racial or ethnic minority.

No, this is about moving past talking about how to understand each other to actually talking to each other. Right now.

That's why there's no agenda to these books other than getting the conversation going. We can discuss studies and methods for elevating social consciousness all we want, but there is no substitute for real dialogue.

That's where Why Are They Like That? stands apart from other books on the topic. You will see how people talk about their real differences of race, religion, sex, disability and more.

The success of the approach is proven: It's based on the ground-breaking Y? website project, blog and column that have attracted millions of visitors and worldwide media attention.

Our hope is that by reading, you will become more comfortable asking and answering the questions yourself, expecting the unexpected in return and helping change the ground rules for how we learn from and about each other. To that end, we wrap up each book in the series with our O.U.T.L.O.U.D. Method for Dialogue, with tips to help you get your own conversations started. Ultimately, that is what this effort is all about.

After all, if you want to make more friends, money and love, you better know the people you're talking to, selling to or opening up to. Knowledge isn't just power. It's all power.

Enjoy.

Phillip J. Milano
Founder, Y?

How do you say "Arab" if you're not from Alabama?

They asked:

Do Middle Easterners find it offensive to be called Arabs or A-rabs?

Karen, white, Staten, N.C.

You said:

A-rab is considered offensive because it is mispronounced. And remember, not all people in the Middle East are Arab. There are Persians (mainly in Iran), Palestinians, Kurd ... it goes on and on. Calling someone from Iran A-rab would really piss them off. Especially because A-rab is how some people in America pronounce it in a derogatory way.

Melanie, 28, white, Chicago

Do not call someone an Arab if he is not an Arab! The best way is to find out what the person calls himself, or find out his country of origin.

Teresa, 21, white, Illinois

Is it Apple or A-pple? Is it I-talian or Italian? The "a" is short in "apple." Pretty simple.

Frank, 38, Hispanic, Los Angeles

If you're an Alabamian from Arab, Ala., it's pronounced with a long A.

Danny, 45, white, South Korea

Call the ones from Saudi Arabia "Saudis." The ones from Iran "Iranians." The ones from Jordan "Jordanians." Get it?

Ann, 38, white, Missouri

We found:

Yes, Arab is pronounced "Ay-rab" when it comes to the town of about 8,000 in Alabama. Outside there, though, that pronunciation distorts how the word is pronounced in Arabic ("Ah-rab"), said Nader Hashemi, director of the Center for Middle East Studies at the University of Denver and author of "Islam, Secularism, and Liberal Democracy" (Oxford University Press).

"If you're being generous, you could forgive it and write it off as someone's accent," he said. "But you also see 'Ay-rab' used by others and in Hollywood films that promote a prejudicial and racial narrative of Muslims. The term becomes associated with a particular offensive representation of Arabs."

Use Middle Easterner as an inclusive catch-all that doesn't invoke religion when describing people from that region, he said. Don't default to "Muslim" (or worse yet, "Moslem"), either, because Jews, Christians and others make their home in the Mideast, too.

Call someone from Iran an "Arab" and there's a good chance they'll be miffed, as most are not Arab, Hashemi said.

"Not only that, but there are ethnic tensions between Iranians and Arabs that go back thousands of years and are now exploited to perpetuate political differences."

Messy stuff, politics.

"Overall, some people are trying to be offensive when they mispronounce, or are showing intellectual laziness from something fossilized in their mind," Hashemi said. "The goal in a changing world should be to find the pronunciation people prefer … to rise to the occasion. When you get it correct phonetically, it can create a very positive impression that you've gone the extra step."

The long and short of American-born Asian children

They asked:

Why are American-born or American-raised Asian children taller than non-American born Asians?

B., 25, Asian, San Diego

You said:

I, too, am taller than my mother and am catching up on my father. My mom agrees I ate much better than she did as a child, partly for financial reasons and partly because her generation had more knowledge about the healthiest foods for their children.

Nicole, 19, Toronto

It may also be growth hormones are finding their way throughout the food chain. When I graduated from high school in 1978, being 6 feet was regarded as tall; now, heights of 6 feet 4 and above are not uncommon.

Augustine, white, Columbia, S.C.

Current knowledge on evolution would say we can't genetically evolve into a population of taller people in just a few generations. So most likely it's that we have had different diets.

Beth, 25, white, United Kingdom

I think it is because the United States is much larger than Vietnam and you get to move around and have different experiences. An example is a goldfish. If you put one in a bowl it will grow to a limit depending on the bowl. Take the fish, and throw it in a lake. The lake is now the limit to how large the fish can grow.

Yan, 28, Asian, Atlanta

Quantity and quality of diet. Traditional cultures were aware of this. Aspiring sumo wrestlers in Japan eat a special high-protein diet in their teens to increase height and weight.

Doug, 31, white, Seattle

We found:

We're just going to go on record here and state we don't think people get taller because they live on a larger landmass. There.

However, they likely do because of diet, said Laura Kelley, who has traveled the world studying culture and cuisine, lectures on Asian food and published the cookbook "The Silk Road Gourmet."

"What we thought were locked-in genetic potentials are turning out to be more plastic," she said.

Asian-Americans aren't the only ones getting taller than their overseas counterparts, but it may seem more pronounced because they're moving from shorter heights of, say, 5 feet 2, to 5 feet 7 in just a generation and a half.

The reason: more protein and calcium in the diet.

"Protein consumption in North America is huge compared to what most Asians even today eat. Eating a half pound of meat is unheard of. They might eat some lamb, and eat the eyeballs, shanks, everything. Here, we eat the muscle and get that nutritional value."

The Western diet and lifestyle is not perfect, of course. There's sugar and fat, and sitting around. A lot.

"We aren't seeing it with Asian-Americans yet, but with Native Americans, as they've moved from indigenous ways, you have seen huge increases in weight and diabetes," Kelley said. "It's also happening in India. As they move to adopting a Western lifestyle, you see an increase in heart disease."

Do Indians have just the deal for you? Don't haggle over it.

They asked, first offer:

Why are people from India always trying to return things to get a better deal, reuse their coupons or use coupons fraudulently?

Tatyanna, white, Illinois

They asked, final offer:

Why do people from India haggle so much? Is there advice on how to deal with these people in a better way?

Doug, Omaha, Neb.

You said:

India is poor, and people have always been taught to save as much as they can.

Pratichi, 18, Indian female, Pune, India

Bartering not only hurts the business, it hurts employees [and] the CEO ...

Sam, Lewisville, Texas

In India, if you bargain, you might get a discount. Most shops here are small operations. Keep calm and tell them it is a fixed price.

Jatin, 32, Indian male, Delhi, India

I am a manager in customer service. ... I believe it's cultural, but I can't stand them, anyway, so I send subordinates to deal with them.

R., 41, white, California

Who wrote this is an ignorant jackass. If you haven't traveled the world to see how others live, it's your problem.

Indian, Connecticut

We found:

Gunjan Bagla of India trade consultant Amritt Ventures (www.theindiaexpert.com) gave us the deal on all this.

Folks in Asia — from Japan to the Mideast and in between — have built relationships based on negotiating for eons, said Bagla, author of "Doing Business in 21st-Century India." Europeans and Americans are the ones doing it a more direct, new way.

"Culturally, it's part of the conversation, and is not considered rude. In fact, a quick transaction is thought cold."

The commerce heritage of India, for example, isn't based on mass-market retail stores but on interacting with small shop owners, he said. That means conversing about value and price.

"There is always that tendency to want to figure out how one can stretch a buck."

Some academics argue that decades of British rule led to impoverishment in India, hence individuals' need to seek value at all turns. And research by the renowned Angus Maddison, professor emeritus of economics at the University of Groningen in The Netherlands until his death in 2010, shows India's share of world GDP dropped from 24 percent in 1700 to less than 3 percent by the time it gained its independence in 1947.

Regarding coupon misuse, some Indians new to the States may see them as a proxy for the dialogue they're used to having with clerks, Bagla said. But folks who state that it's mostly Indians who abuse them may be seeing what they want to see.

"Aberrant behavior ... can get noticed more if it's from someone different from us."

Bottom line: Indians generally seek deals — at all levels, he said. Hard to argue that one, when you consider that in 2006, rather than build a ship, the Indian Navy bought the 35-year-old USS Trenton from the United States for a song — $48.4 million.

The fear of an Asian in your rearview mirror

They asked:

Why do most bad drivers seem to be Asian?

D.M., 26, white male, Vancouver, Canada

You said:

It is a myth. What's more, if you check with someone who works in the auto insurance industry, you will find that Asians have the lowest rate of auto accidents.

Pinny, 19, Asian female, Stockton, Calif.

I cannot drive here in North America. It will take me at least another year to get comfortable with everything on the "wrong" side of the road. Asia entirely drives on the left. Try driving on the left after spending a lifetime doing the exact opposite.

Niti, Pittsburgh

While Asian is an all-encompassing term, I have noticed that in general there is a truth in the question. There seems to be an inability to understand what is going on around them.

S., black male, California

I am Asian and am a horrible driver. I don't know if it is that I can't see all the traffic signs and cars because of my squinty eyes, or because there are usually seven people trying to fit in my Toyota, and it's hard to compensate for the weight. Just joking about all that ... except that I am Asian and don't have a single point on my license.

Daniel, 22, Asian male, Indianapolis

We found:

One need only look at the data to draw conclusions:

California has had big decreases in traffic fatalities in recent years, according to the National Highway Traffic Safety Administration. California has a lot of Asians. Therefore, Asians probably did not get in their cars there in recent years.

Conversely, Alaska had one of the biggest increases in traffic fatalities. It doesn't have a high Asian population. Therefore, again, Asians probably didn't drive a lot there.

Sure, you think we're interpreting statistics to fit misperceptions. Or, you think we should quote these NHTSA findings:

In 2002, only about 2 percent of all Asian deaths were attributable to traffic crashes, about in line with blacks and whites and lower than American Indians and Hispanics. Between 1999 and 2004, Asians had the highest rate of valid licenses. Among drivers killed between 1999 and 2004, other minority groups were as likely as Asians to have had a previous conviction for a crash or speeding and were more likely to have been convicted of a DUI.

To make sense of all this, we found a respected research team: The Good Asian Drivers.

They're a transgender slam poet and lesbian folk-rocker duo who drove themselves on a 30-state tour and caused zero wrecks.

"We're out to break down that and other stereotypes," said Melissa Li, the folkie part of the pair, which also includes Kit Yan. "We've heard all the racist comments — 'Gooks can't ride, your eyes are too small, you can't see to drive ... ' But in fact it was someone else who hit us in L.A.

"I get angry at other drivers, too, but I try not to associate it with race."

Hey, do something about that loud Indian kid, willya?

They asked:

Why do Indians let their kids do what they please? I asked a guy from India why he let his child scream and slam doors, and he said books said you should let your child do as they please.

Rhea, 22, white, Albany, N.Y.

You said:

Looked around lately? Most parents today act like this with their kids … It's not a race issue. It's a society-full-of-crappy-parents issue.

Cassy, 22, white, Jacksonville

Indians do punish their kids …

Sorgul, 20, Kurdish female, Atlanta

I work in a place frequented by a broad range of people. You know which parents don't discipline? White parents, black parents, Indian parents, non-Indian Asian parents, gay parents, straight parents, etc. … And of course, there are parents in all those groups whose children do behave well.

Lynne, Gainesville

We found:

Family therapist Mudita Rastogi does not see a lot of Indian kids throwing tantrums in Albany, N.Y.

OK, her practice is in Arlington Heights, Ill., but still.

Actually, Rastogi, a professor of clinical psychology and a parenting expert with experience in India and the States, didn't blow off the whole notion of Indian parents being more permissive.

"Research says that up to age 5, children in Indian families are indulged more, and the parents are more easygoing," she said.

Here's why: Lots of Indian parents immigrated to the U.S. in recent decades. It was more collectivist where they grew up, and the needs of the family often trumped those of the individual.

"Many were raised to include children in all activities … so most are comfortable being around kids, and expect that they will take part," Rastogi said. "That means people accommodate to their needs."

Take a grocery store meltdown by an Indian tot (not that we've ever seen an American cherub have a hernia by the Despicable Me Fruit Rollups, but work with us). "In a case like that, it might be terrible for a white mom to have her kid cry and say 'I want candy,' but an Indian parent might say, 'Well, the kid was hungry' and look at it from a child-centered perspective."

However, most children of Indian parents who are immigrants adapt to different expectations in America, perhaps behaving one way at school and another at an Indian event, Rastogi said.

Adaptation should go both ways, though.

"How a child appears in public might not be as important as whether the children care about the needs of other family members. Are they considerate of everyone in the family, and willing to share with the extended family? … Many Indian families I know will do anything for their parents."

Therefore, we in the U.S. might examine where our own discomfort comes from on this issue, she said.

"It might be, 'How much can I tolerate something different, as long as the child is not destroying property or doing something unsafe?' We need to ask, 'Why is it bothering me so much?' "

Open up in there: Japanese people and bathrooms

They asked:

I hosted some female Japanese exchange students. I was told I would need to give them a time limit when they go to the bathroom, because they would spend hours in there if they were allowed. I found it to be true. Why do they want to spend hours in the bathroom? What could they be doing?

Dando, Orange, Calif.

You said:

They spend a lot of time in the bathroom because in their culture, bath time is very important, almost religious.

Alex, Atlanta

I spent four years in Japan during the '70s teaching conversational English to young men and women. On several occasions we invited my students to our home to see how we lived and introduce them to our foods (this was way before they discovered American fast foods). The two things the women that visited us found the most interesting were our kitchen with all the "handy" cooking utensils, and our bathroom, where my wife kept all her makeup and other items unique to the American woman. It was like exploring a new world for them. It wouldn't surprise me if it were still the same. The cooking area and bathroom in Japan were quite simple compared to ours.

Frank, 60, California

We found:

Holy shiitake, they've taken over the car market, now they're taking over our bathrooms.

But really, just as with some American teens, some young girls from Japan really can "fall in" if they're left to their own devices in an American bathroom, says Thomas Snitch, a long-time business and government consultant who specializes in U.S.-Asian affairs.

"We just had two exchange girls here from Japan. It was unbelievable, the shower would run for an hour," he said. "Part of it is that when you're living in, say, Tokyo, in tiny apartments, as young girls they have limited private time in front of the mirror or in the shower. So they think it's a luxury to have your own washroom and be able to close the door and run hot water as long as you want. … I was tempted to say, 'What the hell is going on in there?' "

And let's talk about those Japanese bathrooms.

They are very tiny, with something akin to a small tub to soak in, Snitch said.

And bathing, well, it's just different over there.

"In Japan, there's cleaning, and then there's soaking. You clean yourself before getting into the tub. Soaking in very hot water is a very serious ritual. It is popular at Japanese spas and is very communal, like cleansing the mind and soul."

Then there are the toilets.

"Over there, they are fantastic, with heated seats and washing and drying jets," Snitch said. "The Japanese can be fascinated with gadgetry. You need a master's degree to know how to turn these things on. Some public ones even have an 'Otohime,' which mimics the sound of flushing water to mask any real noise."

These high-end porcelain babies are now making their way to the United States.

"For a Westerner who gets one and hits the wrong button, they're in for a surprise."

What should she expect traveling around India?

They asked:

I am an outspoken female leaving for India. Is there anything I should be worried about, such as covering my face or how I dress, drinking at bars, etc.? I do not want to offend anyone, and I do not want to put myself in danger.

Marie, 22, Tampa

You said:

I moved to India when I was 20 and experienced a minimum of sexual harassment. My advice: do not wear low-cut shirts, halter tops or shorts. You do not have to cover your face or hair. I found Indian men on the whole to be caring and helpful.

Lisa, 25, Los Angeles

There is something called "eve teasing," when men will harass you on the street. Some Indian women carry stickpins with them to poke rude men.

P. Kitty, 38, Caribou, Maine

It doesn't matter what you wear (in India), if people know you're a foreigner and are not educated about other cultures, they will sexually harass you.

Diana, 18, Sacramento, Calif.

I take strong exception to what Diana says. Most people here are good-natured and very helpful. Nobody will try to harass you sexually unless you invite it yourself.

Padmanabhan, 31, Chennai, India

The farther south you go, the more polite it gets. Bombay and Bangalore are cosmopolitan, and women move freely without fear. These places also have pretty cool discos/nightclubs. As long as you are with company, you should be safe.

Zip, 30, Hindu male, Birmingham, Ala.

We found:

This would be easier if Marie were more specific and hadn't asked about the seventh-largest land mass on Earth (1.27 million square miles) that holds a sixth of the world's population (about 1.2 billion people). For example, hit us with "If I go to a guy named Ajith's place about 2 1/2 blocks off Shanghumugham Beach near Thiruvananthapuram at 8 p.m. next Thursday, will I be harassed?" and maybe we can start running some background checks.

Sadly, harassment of women in India, including domestic violence, stalking, acid attacks, dowry battery and rapes, has made headlines. Some studies suggest nearly seven in 10 women in India suffer domestic violence. An infamous gang rape in New Delhi shocked the nation and highlighted longstanding abuse of females. The Indian Parliament has passed new laws protecting women from sexual violence and strengthening penalties, but the matter is far from settled.

We talked to Max Ali, director of group operations at SITA World Tours in Los Angeles, a top India tour operator, about what travelers should expect.

He didn't out India as running rabid with groping guys. In fact, the little massive country that could is growing rapidly — economically and culturally.

"Indian guys are interested in Western women, but they are not aggressive, by American standards," he said, adding that in big cities, U.S. women won't even stand out at the bars.

"But in smaller towns, it's best to dress modestly and maintain a lower profile. No short-shorts, and with blouses, a little bit of cleavage, not a lot."

As with anywhere, there are still "backward areas" of the country where men might ogle and harass, Ali said.

"But I would have to go searching for something like that to find it," he said.

He's chomping at the bit to ask about Filipinos eating loudly

They asked:

I live in an area with a large Filipino population. Most of them smack their lips when eating — and not quietly. Is this common to the Filipino culture and not considered rude?

Mike, 43, Santa Cruz, Calif.

You said:

I am married to a Filipina. It's cultural. Filipinos, as well as others from that part of the world, will smack their lips. A host will perceive this as a subtle sign that her meal is good.

Jerry, 54, white, Houston

I grew up in the Philippines and was taught it was impolite to make any sounds while having a meal (other than scintillating conversation). Rude is rude in any society. These notions often disguise biases that reinforce our "otherness" and condone our marginalization.

Gerry, Filipino male, New York

Many times I have had my meal ruined by Asians sitting next to me chewing with their mouths open, sloshing their food around in their mouths, making slurping and lip-smacking sounds. Why can't they adopt our habits?

Lucy, New York

Most Filipinos I know chew with their mouths closed.

Eduardo, Manila, Philippines

I am Filipino. Slurping soup from a cup or small bowl usually does not offend most people of Filipino descent when done in the proper setting, such as in your own home or in the company of friends. But I don't consider it part of the culture to "eat loudly."

B.C., Northern California

We found:

So, is it a thrilla in Manila when folks sit down to eat?

The clacking can get cacophonous as Filipinos attack a meal with family or friends — but more so in the Philippines than here, says Gerry Gelle, author of Filipino Cuisine: Recipes from the Islands.

It can even become a contest, with the men trying to outsmack one another, he added.

"It doesn't matter whether it's urban or rural, or a high-crust or low-crust crowd, they are all smacking," Gelle said. "But it's more than likely a group of them by themselves."

In a mixed environment or a corporate setting, most know better than to chew with their mouths open, he said.

The reason for the ruckus at other times is that, well, who says you have to be quiet when you eat, anyway?

"In Europe, for example, it was royalty that set the dining rules. But the rules for eating are more family-oriented in Asia. You can eat with your mouth open. No one has ever said not to."

Food, and having enough of it, is a big deal in the East, so many people lip-smack just to let others know that "yeah, I'm here at the table, and I'm eating," Gelle said.

Lines are drawn in the tablecloth, though.

"Nope, no belching when your plate is clear. That's a Northern European thing," he said. "And while they eat their noodles in one long slurp in Japan — you never break them with your lips because the noodle is a symbol of life — we Filipinos do cut our noodles."

Are Japanese people really into being in the photo?

They asked:

I have been many places in the world. On several occasions, Japanese people have asked me to snap a picture of them. Be it at the Grand Canyon, Pompeii or Tulum, I am handed a camera and take a picture of them standing in front of the attraction. What is this obsession with self?

John, 48, Cincinnati

You said:

It's to show that you were there and enjoyed yourself. I don't think it's about "self."

Krista Y., 23, Nagoya, Japan

I am Filipino. My mother says pictures should always be taken of yourself near a sign of your location. She says it shows you have been at a certain place and have the picture to prove it. Last picture I took was at Niagara Falls, and Mom made sure to tell me it wasn't close up enough to read the sign!

Janet, 38, Conover, Ohio

There's a slightly more complex answer involving the isolationist nature of Japan, the supposed freedom of being able to leave an island where 60-hour work weeks are the norm, and the desire to keep memories of their "escape" as handy as possible. But I think the professor who taught me that is full of it.

Juno, 21, Asian male, Richmond, Va.

It is not just the Japanese who do this. Everywhere I've gone, I've seen people of all races, ethnicities and backgrounds very casually and politely ask a stranger to photograph them at an attraction. It ain't just the Japanese. Besides, have you ever seen a people more self-focused than us Americans?

Michael, Falls Church, Va.

We found:

Really, can't a shot of El Capitan in Yosemite be improved upon with your happy mug in front of it, selfie or not?

"The Japanese and many in East Asia have a fascination with electronic gadgets, and using cell phone cameras is one way they, in general, express their individuality," said David Matsumoto, psychology professor at San Francisco State University and author of The New Japan: Debunking Seven Cultural Stereotypes.

More specifically, getting themselves into their photos really helps get across that sense of self, he added.

Why the need?

Picture it: Tiny island. Tons of people. Limited resources and land to grow food. It all adds up to a society where rules and rigidity became important in order for the group to survive, Matsumoto said.

"You can't have a free-for-all. So there are a lot of unspoken rules in Japanese culture … and there can be social isolation if you are too different, so some people will do other things to not conform," he said. "So if they go to the Grand Canyon, the focal point of the photo is still on themselves. There is a need to shine meaning on the individual existence."

Folks in Japan are also big on nostalgia, he added.

"The culture looks back at the goodness of the past. Again, because there's so much conformity in present-day life, people have a need to find uniqueness. Looking back on experiences through photos is one way to fulfill that need."

What's with the red dot on their foreheads?

They asked:

Why do Indian women wear a red dot on their foreheads?

Aprile, 23, Holiday

You said:

In North India, women wear a bindi after they are married. In other parts, the bindi is put on the forehead after praying to God. It is considered as a sign of his blessings.

K., 25, Asian female, San Francisco

It's a kind of fashion now. Shania Twain has put a dot on her forehead in her song "From This Moment On." It also makes us different from the rest of the world because no other country uses it.

Roshni, Virginia Beach, Va.

My Indian friend says it's traditional, decorative, Indian jewelry.

Andy, 17, Asian, Jacksonville

You can get all types of pretty ones at Indian markets.
Sarita, Indian, Apex, N.C.

It's in their religion. It's like asking whites why do nuns wear that outfit.

Jasmeen, 18, Muslim, Chicago

Hindi women wear it as a chakra symbol representing the third eye, the eye that sees into oneself.

Sezu, Williams, Tenn.

It was once used more for ritual and caste-related significances but now is more for fashion purposes.

Julie, 18, Canada

We found:

We're just all over the place on this, aren't we? How to connect the dots?

Samar Sardana runs visionsofindia.com and sells bindis — a word that comes from the Sanskrit "bindu," for dot or drop.

The bindi is purely a forehead decoration and is often stick-on felt or jewelry, he said. It shouldn't be confused with a tilak, a traditional Hindu mark created with powder or paste that symbolizes marriage or has religious significance. A lot of Hindu men and women don't even wear the tilak anymore, but more women — Hindu or not — are getting their bindi on. His site sells them for anywhere from 35 cents for a nine-pack of basic bindis to up to $5.69 for a one- to 15-pack of ornate ones. Younger people, a lot of them into belly-dancing, get them.

"It's a fashion statement, for decoration, and not just for Indian women," he said. "Gwen Stefani and Madonna wear them."

What about all the mystical stuff — the third eye, Hindu gods, enlightenment and all that?

"They say the tilak is for the third eye and has to do with the sixth chakra in the forehead, the seat of concealed wisdom, balance and power," Sardana said. "I don't believe all that. And most who wear a bindi wouldn't even know about it."

Do Asians all look alike? Hard to say ... and see

They asked:

How do you differentiate between different Asians, i.e. Korean, Japanese, Filipino, Vietnamese, etc.?

Rachel, 36, white, Canada

You said:

Good luck. I'm Asian and I can barely tell. What complicates matters is intermarriage between different ethnicities. Also, the Chinese have migrated throughout history to many parts of Asia, giving their genetic material to other people.

Siggy, Newport Beach, Calif.

Generally people from mainland China or Korea tend to be a little taller, have the stereotypical "squinty" Asian eyes and are fairer. Southern Asians are shorter, darker-skinned and have larger, round eyes. Vietnamese people tend to be pretty fair, with large eyes, but they tend to be quite small on average, and Japanese people are also fairly short and tend to be fairer, with squinty eyes.

J., 21, Asian, Canada

Environment plays a big part, too. For example, Koreans or Chinese who were born or raised in Japan look very Japanese, and the ethnic Japanese who were left in China as infants after World War II look very Chinese. And Japanese-Americans, especially third- or fourth-generation, look different from Japanese people in Japan because they have grown up speaking English, smiling and laughing like Americans, and this shows in their facial expressions and behavior.

David, 35, Eurasian, Tokyo

We found:

Try as we did to sweet-talk UCLA anthropologist Kyeyoung Park into making massive generalizations about physical differences among Asian subgroups, we only got a few.

"It's not easy to tell differences among Asians," she said. "Race is not scientifically valid, and there's so much overlap that I can't really generalize with much accuracy."

Darn. Nonetheless:

— Vietnamese-Americans do tend to be somewhat taller than their counterparts in Vietnam, which Park theorizes might be from a better diet in the U.S.

— Some Koreans and Chinese can have rounder faces than other Asians.

— Southern Chinese are shorter and thinner; northern Chinese are taller, as are Koreans.

While physiological differences can be hard to pin down, differences in appearance that occur because of culture, economics or migration are easier to pick out, she said.

For example, the Japanese were among the first Asians to become more affluent and take on Western styles, and it showed in their hair, makeup, style of dress and more. Then Koreans, who were under Japanese colonial rule from 1910-1945, came into their own and began to catch up.

Now the trend is to retain ethnicity and not go for Westernization, Park noted.

"Even in plastic surgery, in the past they would ask doctors to make them look like a Western model. But now patients are asking to keep their look, not having eyelid surgery, or if they have their nose done, they don't want a 'high' nose anymore — they just want to improve it."

Are there vacancies, and is there a Patel behind the front desk?

They asked:

Why are so many Indian people either owners or managers of independent motels, and why do a large percentage have the last name "Patel"?

Dick A., Santa Rosa, Calif.

You said:

One or two families get their foot in the door, then through hard work, networking, informal credit and pooling resources they get their brothers, sisters, cousins, friends and relatives involved. Before long, a certain ethnic group seems to "dominate" a certain type of business. There is no conspiracy or devious plan involved.

Mihir, 25, Indian-American male, Illinois

Patels are businesspeople, so wherever they go they continue to do what they know, and what they are taught is their place in society. But not all Indians own hotels and 7-Elevens.

Avanti, 18, Asian female, Mississippi

The typical immigrant family has one major asset: a willingness to put the whole family to work. You want people you can trust at the cash register. You make a go of it, and perhaps bring other relatives over and help them set up. In a similar way, my father became an accountant because he had relatives who were successful accountants at a time when jobs were scarce.

Jerry, 52, New Britain, Conn.

We found:

A Patel play-by-play, translated from an abysmal phone conversation but highly successful e-mail exchange with researcher Govind Bhakta, author of Patels: A Gujarati Community History in the United States (UCLA Asian American Studies Press):

— Family names aren't a huge deal for a lot of Indians.

— For lack of a better surname, some choose the caste to which they belong.

— People of the same caste often inter-marry.

Voila — in the heavily populated Gujarat State in India, where Patel is a big caste, there are about 40 million Patels.

Taking it further:

— Immigration reforms in the United States brought a lot of Patels here in the '60s (there are about 2 million today).

— To adjust to a strange new land, they sought work where their families could stay together in one place.

— Older Americans at the time who ran independent motels were looking to retire and get out of the business.

— Many Patels were keen businesspeople.

Boom — they took over these operations and kept costs low by hiring other Patels, whom they then helped to open their own franchises, leading to many flourishing Patel-owned motels.

Bam — as recently at the 1980s, law enforcement officials embarked on a fruitless probe to find a "Patel crime family" modeled on the Italian mafia.

Pressing on:

— Over the years, second- and third-generation Patels have diversified into many other fields.

— Many are now teachers, engineers, electronics workers or health care employees.

Bam again — the Patel-owned motel phenomenon has probably peaked.

She'd like to nail down what Chinese salon workers are saying

They asked:

I find it very rude when I go into a nail salon and all the Chinese workers start speaking to each other in Chinese. If you come to our country, shouldn't you be learning our language?

Rhea, 22, white, Albany, N.Y.

You said:

I agree. Listening to immigrants chatter in other languages is highly annoying. It makes me feel invisible.

Sherry, black, Fort Worth

They are not trying to be rude. Sometimes they feel embarrassed because their English might not sound right. If this stops you from going to an Asian nail salon, then we are better off not having rude customers like yourself.

Eastern, Cheney, Wash.

As long as you're getting what you paid for, who cares what they say?

Peter, 21, black, Jacksonville

Why would you spend your hard-earned money somewhere you are not comfortable? As a black person I often go into businesses that make me uncomfortable. I leave and do not go back.

Jack, 31, Johnson, Ala.

Let's give a little respect for these hard-working individuals. We are a nation of immigrants. Some people act as if their nail tech is invisible. Speak to that person holding your hand!

Patty, 50, white, Jacksonville

We found:

Darn right it would be rude for an Asian nail tech to speak Chinese in front of you. The least they could do is give you the respect of confusing you in Vietnamese, their likely mother tongue.

Almost 40 percent of the 380,635 licensed nail techs in the United States are Vietnamese, according to a survey by the trade publication Nails. About two-thirds of the 1,868 nail salons registered in Florida alone are owned by Vietnamese-Americans, says Tin Nguyen, director of the Vietnamese Nail Care Professional Association.

Should they use English when they feign interest in your kid's soccer game?

"We recognize that clients often feel uneasy when nail techs speak their native language," Nguyen said. "We discourage that type of behavior. But it often is difficult. Most Vietnamese nail techs don't speak English besides a few words like 'Hello' or 'What can I do for you?' "

Hannah Lee, associate publisher of Nails Magazine (nailsmag.com), said Vietnamese immigrants took to the nail tech business about 25 years ago because it didn't require them to speak English and didn't require a lot of startup money to open a salon.

Yes, they should probably speak more English if they know it, Lee said, but no, they're not talking about you or making fun of you when they speak their native language — one investigative reporter who spoke fluent Vietnamese tested that by pretending not to know the language and found the techs were just chatting with each other.

"Lighten up, you're getting a salon service at a price less than half the average of a regular salon, so you're kind of getting what you pay for."

Cats not the secret ingredient in your Pu Pu Platter

They asked:

To Chinese people or people who work in Chinese restaurants: Do you kill cats, cook them and sell them to your customers, stating that it is chicken?

Elizabeth S., 23, mixed race, Philadelphia

You said:

Cat (or dog) meat does not taste like chicken. Cats and dogs are inefficient sources of protein. They are much more expensive than pork or chicken. In China, they are served on special occasions, and not everyone can afford them or has a preference for them. They are not served in North America as chicken because of the cost. Chinese living in America also understand the taboo against eating cat or dog meat in this culture.

Leonard, 45, Asian, Tampa

There are animals that are raised for food, and then there are pets. One should not eat pets.

Katherine, 22, Asian, Toronto

My wife is Filipina, and I've visited that country with her many times. She tells me that only the very poor and desperate eat dog meat, much like some poorer people in this country used to eat horse meat.

A.C.C., male, West Lafayette, Ind.

Icelandic people eat putrefied shark meat and pickled ram testicles. Thais are rumored to eat cockroaches. Northern Chinese enjoy turtle soup. Kenyans eat monkey brains. Koreans used to eat dog, although the younger generation, having adopted Western values, considers it low-class and barbaric. Anyway, the list goes on and on. Not just Asians eat funky stuff. White people and black people around the world do, too.

Jake, 20, Korean-American, Los Angeles

We found:

Tongue got your cat?

Actually, there's no need to fear that your fave feline will wind up in a takeout box as Egg Foo Fluffy.

This tale has been wending its way across the urban legend landscape for more than 100 years, much of it due to a good old-fashioned fear of foreigners, says Gail de Vos, a University of Alberta professor and author of Tales, Rumors, and Gossip: Exploring Contemporary Folk Literature (Libraries Unlimited).

"Look at a cat. How much meat is there?" she said. "I'm not sure why there is this rumor about Chinese restaurants. Maybe it's because meat [in Chinese cuisine] is cut so finely ... in tiny chunks."

The stereotype sometimes pops up when there are news reports of a local Chinese restaurant closing.

"It's a racist reaction. Because [Chinese restaurant owners] are different, we can tend to distrust what they are giving us. And today we are more insular than we used to be. Despite the Web and TV, we are still terrified of things that are different."

It is true that dogs and cats don't enjoy exalted-pet status in all countries. And while cats are eaten in some far-flung areas of China and dog meat is served in Korea, these practices are waning, de Vos added. They certainly aren't followed in North America or Europe among Asians or Asian-Americans, she stressed.

Beyond the pale: What do South Asians think about skin tone?

They asked:

South Asia is very poor. Many South Asians are as dark as black people. So why are most Indians and other South Asians outside of Asia so arrogant, especially toward blacks?

Alison, 23, Afro-Caribbean, New York

You said:

My South Asian friends aren't arrogant. Your problem might be your attitude, because you make a lot of generalizations about South Asians.

Michelle, 23, black, Fort Worth, Texas

This sort of racism exists in India, too, where men prefer lighter-skinned brides. Also, the media doesn't portray a very positive picture of black people in America.

Amita, Asian, Mumbai, India

Alison: I have noticed the same thing. I think they act this way because white people tell foreigners when they come to the United States that it is OK to treat black people like trash.

Chris, black, Waldorf, Md.

White people do not tell South Asians to denigrate black people when they come to this country. What do you think, there are secret info sessions for Indians and Pakistanis when they immigrate where white people tell them what's up?

Todd, Washington, D.C.

I'm from the sub-continent. In South Asia you would get discriminated against, most importantly on skin color. It goes back a few thousand years, when the Aryans entered India. They invented the caste system, which put them at the top and [darker-skinned] locals at the bottom. Almost everyone there has the same view: black should be kept away from white. Not all South Asians think like this, but generally they do.

Asian male, 21, Australia

We found:

After weeks of interview requests were greeted with silence from Asian-Indian societies, professors and Indian political groups, we got the message: People aren't dying to talk about this one.

Undeterred, we called New York attorney Nandini N. Ramnath, who's done work for Human Rights Watch and took heat for a Beliefnet.com essay in which she rapped Indians and Hindus for prejudiced attitudes about skin color.

While most Indians born in America don't harbor condescending "wink-wink, hush-hush" attitudes about darker skin, it's not always the case for older Indians, many of whom arrived here with little and worked hard to succeed, said Ramnath, who is second-generation.

"There's a real lack of understanding. ... As much as it was difficult to find a job and get settled, they still didn't have a legacy of racial discrimination here that hindered their performance in the way it can hinder African-Americans."

One need only look to popular skin-lightening creams in South Asia such as Unilever's "Fair & Lovely" to see how entrenched views in the homeland are about the allure of paler skin, Ramnath added.

"Even my mother told me 'Don't go in the sun, you'll get dark and won't be attractive.' I said 'Mom, I'm going to the beach and there's nothing you can say about it.'"

Ah, those tiny, submissive, exotic Asian females...

They asked:

My friends and I are always curious about what kind of Asian girls foreigners think are beautiful.

Ying-Yao, 24, Asian female, Miami

You said:

I'd say it's just the "exotic" aspect of them to the Western imagination. We have a long history of imagining the mysterious Asian, however mistaken that may be.

Vail, 40, male, Philadelphia

For me, the petite body and jet-black hair are the big attracters. Asian women [also] have very developed sexual identities. Also, I believe Asian women are educated and articulate.

Keith, 42, white male, Jacksonville

I think the real draw is the myth that Asian girls are comfortable in a subservient position. I've dated a couple of Asian girls, and neither were anything resembling subservient. But I do have to admit that — at first — I was attracted to the "unusualness" factor: They were something other than the blond-haired, blue-eyed girls of my hometown.

Mike T., white male, Grand Rapids, Mich.

We found:

Stereotypes about the exotic, submissive Asian woman have floated around the United States since at least the mid-1800s, said Guofang Li, a professor of second language and literacy education at Michigan State University.

When Chinese women first came to this country, many were concubines (secondary wives) for Chinese men, she noted. The cliched image of the meek, available Asian beauty carried over into modern society, particularly among some white males.

"It fits their psychological needs in terms of looking for an ideal woman," Li said. "There are those who don't look at Asian women as who they are individually."

Nowadays, nearly six of 10 Asian women in the United States are in the labor force — the same rate as women overall — and their median earnings are 14 percent higher than for all women, according to the U.S. Census.

Still, Asian women appear to be a popular match with American — particularly Caucasian — men. The U.S. Census estimates that there are 578,000 married couples in the United States in which one spouse was white and the other Asian, the highest of any interracial category.

Ming Tan, a Chinese-American writer and self-described "Asian relationship expert," angered many Asian-Americans with her book How to Attract Asian Women (Asian Socials Inc.). Her list of reasons for why Asian women might be attractive reads like a Top 10 list of stereotypes, among them that they tend to look younger and thinner than other women and are less materialistic.

The bottom line, though, is that Asian women moved beyond such broad-brush characterizations and gender hierarchy rules long ago, Li stressed.

"Many white men simply underestimate our achievements," she said.

You may not know squat about the Middle East

They asked:

I often see pictures of Middle Eastern men, usually lower class, squatting on the ground. I haven't seen other men do this, and it seems like there are other positions that would be more comfortable, even if they did not have access to a chair. Any ideas on why this is?

Anne, 22, Cedar Falls, Iowa

You said:

Squatting is comfortable, and other than standing or sitting, I don't know of any other position that would work. Most parts of the Middle East where pictures like that are taken are hot and dry. If you sit on hot and dry dirt or sand, it's uncomfortable. It burns your bum, and the seat of your pants gets dirty. It's usually not very practical to carry a chair around, so sitting is out. Standing works for a while, until you want a break, thus the squatting. As for the lower class doing this, unless you're wealthy enough to have someone running around after you with a chair on his back, that's the standard for most economic classes.

A. Schurman, 27, female, Ammon, Idaho

I don't think it's just in the Middle East that people squat. In the United States it would probably be seen as vulgar or odd — unless you escape society and enter the forests. Most forest people do squat. It stretches your back out nicely and keeps your bottom clean if it's just rained and the log seats around the campfire are wet, as is the ground. And it makes for good, um, No. 2's? Really, it does! Our toilets are one of the worst things for our colons. As someone who lived many years in America's wilderness, I'd say it's pretty common here, too.

Jessica, Jacksonville

We found:

Ah, the forest people. We'd forgotten about them, dismissed them, laughed off their squatting capabilities and pleasures.

We did not, however, forget about occupational therapist people, one of whom knows more than diddly about squatting Middle Eastern and Asian people.

Over the course of a decade and many trips to Asia and India, Susan Mulholland, professor of occupational therapy at the University of Alberta, reviewed residents' range of motion, in part for a company that makes artificial hips and knees and wanted to know how flexible folks over there were.

It turns out, quite.

They're good at things like squatting, and they like it.

"It is more common among lower-income people," Mulholland said. "They tend to not have furniture, the women are cooking over a fire, closer to the ground ... you don't have toilets — that's a high-end commodity. You bathe by the river. You crouch down to the water source."

In the West and in colder climates, people are more concerned about dirt on the ground, and so "we've raised ourselves above it," she said. Plus, North Americans' roots are mainly European, where the chair was developed. It elevated a person — say, a king — above others. Hence our cultural aversion to the "low" life.

"But over there, to have an 80-year-old woman squatting is normal. In our culture, God forbid my grandmother would get near the floor. [In Asia] you are raised near the ground, and continue to have that flexibility."

The O.U.T.L.O.U.D. Method to Dialogue

OPEN UP: This is mostly about opening up to yourself. Why do you want to engage someone? Is it for the right reasons? The answers might help you figure out how to approach another person. A friend once told me the real reason I started Y? wasn't for me to learn more about "Buddhists in Asia or lesbians in San Francisco," but because I wanted to learn something more about myself. He was right. Acknowledging that has helped give me perspective when considering others' answers.

USE YOUR HEAD: Plan for the right question. Not all questions need to be the "wet dogs" variety. Stereotypes and clichés don't work as well as sincere attempts to talk.

TIME IT RIGHT: Create the "O.U.T.L.O.U.D. Moment". Pick your spots for provocative dialogue. Find a genuine opening rather than create a false one. It's often during those down times between all the "vital" discourse that we can most easily find a direct path to someone's point of view. If you spend enough time sitting in the cubicle next to someone of a different culture, chances are there'll come a time — over food, perhaps, or during a power outage — when the topic you've been dying to broach will wend its way naturally into the discussion.

LOCK IN ON THE TARGET: Keeping things simple can give the best chance for getting another's trust and a meaningful reply. Some of the best questions at Y?, those that prompt the most telling answers, are also often the easiest to digest. Remember, it's not about winning your point. It's what comes from the heart that counts most — and captures people's interest. Talking from the heart also means easing into things by letting someone know *why* it would help you to learn the answer to your question before you ask it.

OWN UP TO ASSUMPTIONS: One of the most refreshing and repetitive surprises of the Y? project is the difficulty in predicting how a person will respond to a question. Blacks do not think in lockstep. Nor do whites. Nor Christians or Muslims. Nor gays or straights. Be receptive to another's ideas. Wipe the slate clean and listen to the content of the message, not the color or culture of the messenger.

UNLOAD YOUR EXPECTATIONS: Many of us are thinner-skinned than we'll admit. When we get hit with an answer or comment we hadn't anticipated, our emotions can often get caught off-balance, and our egos get bruised. The solution: Expect the unexpected. You'll never be blindsided or taken aback by information that doesn't gibe with your worldview.

DIGEST THE DIALOGUE: Learning about others doesn't stop when the talking's over. Assess what you're told and how it fits with or departs from your perspectives. Recap your discussion with a third party to distill the most relevant information into its most meaningful points.

ABOUT THE AUTHOR

Phillip J. Milano is the founder of Y? The National Forum on People's Differences, the acclaimed cross-cultural dialogue project that encourages people to ask unflinching, politically incorrect questions about our differences.

Since its creation in 1998, Phillip's website, YForum.com, has attracted millions of visitors and thousands of questions and answers. He has been featured on CBS, CNN, BET and the BBC, and in numerous newspapers, including The Washington Post, New York Times and USA Today.

He is the author of the Perigee book "I Can't Believe You Asked That!" as well as writer of the pioneering newspaper column/blog "Dare to Ask."

Mr. Milano is a 25-year newspaper veteran. He received his Masters of Business Administration from Northern Illinois University and his Bachelors of Science in Journalism from Southern Illinois University.

SPEECHES AND APPEARANCES

Mr. Milano is an in-demand speaker. For bookings, contact

Contemporary Issues Agency
809 Turnberry Drive, Waunakee, WI 53597-2256
Phone: 800-843-2179
Fax: 608-849-6311
CIAspeakers.com
Info@CIAspeakers.com